# Bionic Butterfly

Written and Illustrated by
Matt Whitlock

FaithKidz®

*Equipping Kids for Life*

An Imprint of Cook Communications Ministries
Colorado Springs, CO

Faith Parenting Guide

Ages
4-7

Respect

A Faith Parenting Guide
can be found starting on page 32.

Faith Kidz is an imprint of Cook Communications Ministries
Colorado Springs, Colorado 80918
Cook Communications, Paris, Ontario
Kingsway Communications Ltd, Eastbourne, England

Bionic Butterfly ©2005 by Matt Whitlock

All rights reserved. No part of this publication may be reproduced without written permission, except for brief quotations in books and critical reviews. For information, write
Cook Communications Ministries, 4050 Lee Vance View, Colorado Springs, CO 80918.

All Scripture quotations, unless indicated, are taken from the NEW INTERNATIONAL
VERSION®. NIV®. Copyright ©1995, 1996, 1998 by International Bible Society. Used by
permission of Zondervan Publishing House. All rights reserved.

First printing, 2005
Printed in Hong Kong
1 2 3 4 5  Printing/Year 09 08 07 06 05

ISBN: 0781440610

Editor: Heather Gemmen
Illustrator: Matt Whitlock
Designer: RJS Design Studio

# For my mom, Mary W.

Thanks also to:
Andrea Christian, Jayne
Andrews, Arnel Platon,
Marty Cummins,
and Jenny

Billy was one
very sad little bug
because of that bully,
Stinky the Slug.

4

The slug took his lunch money each afternoon.
Poor Billy was helpless against this big goon!

"**F**eeling bad Billy Boy? It's not the end!"

Sure enough it was Clark, his glory-hog friend.

"Tell me your troubles. There's no cause to pout.

I'm sure *I'll* think of a way to help out!"

6

As you'll see, Clark was not like most guys.
He wanted a chance to wear his disguise!
When a hero was needed, Clark slipped away,
changed into his outfit, to come save the day!

"Bionic Butterfly" would bust out with wings,
flying around doing hero-type things.
He'd find a lost puppy, help a cat off the roof.
Then he'd strut all around, like a butterfly goof.

Clark wanted that bully to pay for his crime,

but his fine hero plan would take lots of time.

So as Billy went home, Clark started to scheme

of TV reporters who'd cover the scene.

Billy told Dad that Stinky was cruel.
Could Mother excuse him
    (*pleeease*) from school?
He begged and he pleaded
    with lots of good reasons.
He should skip school for years—
    or at least 'til next season.

But Dad said, "You can't hide
from bullies forever.
To stop them you have to be
courageous and clever!
On this slug I'd use
the old Golden Rule.
If that doesn't work,
tell your teacher at school."

"This Golden Rule
must be a new move
with flying feet and fancy kung fu!
I can slam this slug
with a mean judo chop!
What is the secret?"
Billy asked of his pop.

14

"**S**lam-banging Stinky Slug
won't make things right.

Don't let that anger
cause you to fight.

Treat him instead
like you wish
he'd treat you.

It's certainly right—
but not easy to do."

His dad's Golden Rule left Billy dumbfounded.
This plan was certain to get him *so* pounded!
"I'll get creamed either way," he said with a sigh.
So young Billy Bug thought he'd give it *one* try.

In the meanwhile, Clark is adjusting his suit,
He looks like a hero from his cape to his boots.
He calls the reporters from the five o'clock news
and tells them to show up with camera crews.

The next day Billy went back to his classes.

Immediately Stinky knocked off his glasses!

"Now gimme that lunch money!" Stinky Slug said,

"Or maybe you want to get bonked on the head!"

"I have something for you, but no money today."
Billy picked up his glasses, then turned away!
Grabbing his backpack, he pulled out a tin,
"Snack on this, Stinky!" he said with a grin.

The confused Stinky Slug didn't know what to do.
"You gave me some candy after I beat on you?"
Bill said, "Let's be friends, not continue to fight.
I'd rather have fun than run for my life!"

Stinky Slug smiled a slimy slug grin.
No one had wanted to be friends with him!
They turned to go out to play with a ball
but jumped when they heard a thunderous call.

"**I**'m coming! I'm coming!
    You don't need to fear!
Bionic Butterfly is finally here!"
He swooped and he turned
    and drew a big crowd.
As he touched down he hollered out loud.

"Watch, everyone,
    as I save good old Billy!"
But since they were friends now,
    Clark just sounded silly.
The Golden Rule had stopped all the fights
    and Clark just looked funny
wearing those tights!

# Bionic Butterfly

### Ages: 4-7

**Life Issue:** I want my children to treat others with kindness, even when they don't seem to deserve it.

### Spiritual Building Block: Respect

Do the following activities to help your child understand why kindness is important.

 **Sight:** Go out for a nature walk with your child and try to spot butterflies and cocoons. Ask your child to name other transformations that occur in nature (for example, changing seasons, changing leaves, growing up, and so on). Explain how God can cause changes on both the outside and inside of things—and that he can do the same in us. With God's help, we can find love in our hearts for bullies and mean kids when it would seem nearly impossible without his help.

# Bionic Butterfly

**Ages:** 4-7

**Life Issue:** I want my children to treat others with kindness, even when they don't seem to deserve it.

**Spiritual Building Block:** Respect

Do the following activities to help your child understand why kindness is important.

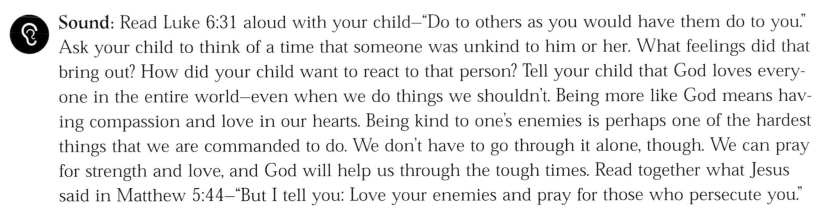

**Sound:** Read Luke 6:31 aloud with your child—"Do to others as you would have them do to you." Ask your child to think of a time that someone was unkind to him or her. What feelings did that bring out? How did your child want to react to that person? Tell your child that God loves everyone in the entire world—even when we do things we shouldn't. Being more like God means having compassion and love in our hearts. Being kind to one's enemies is perhaps one of the hardest things that we are commanded to do. We don't have to go through it alone, though. We can pray for strength and love, and God will help us through the tough times. Read together what Jesus said in Matthew 5:44—"But I tell you: Love your enemies and pray for those who persecute you."

# Bionic Butterfly

Ages: 4-7

**Life Issue:** I want my children to treat others with kindness, even when they don't seem to deserve it.

**Spiritual Building Block:** Respect

Do the following activities to help your child understand why kindness is important.

**Touch:** Make a homemade superhero costume with your child. You could use a bed sheet as a cape and strips of aluminum foil for wristbands. Explain that Luke 6:31 is often called the Golden Rule and why it is so important to follow. To emphasize this message, write the verse on a strip of masking tape and tape the 'rule' to a ruler. It can double as a "superhero sword" with your child's costume and will serve as a constant reminder for him or her to follow the Golden Rule.

# Add These Fun Titles from Matt Whitlock to Your Child's Library!

## Fleas and Thank You
*A Story about Politeness*

If kids have to learn about being polite, this is the way to do it! The zany world of artist and author Matt Whitlock comes to life as he boldly exposes the under-appreciated world of fleas and their favorite game show. Even the youngest children will be enchanted as they learn along with Penelope Flea the rewards of politeness.

ISBN: 0-78144-062-9   ITEM #: 103314   10 x 8   HC   36P

## Hear No Weevil
*A Story about Temptation*

Children learn about the creepy bug–Mr. Fibface Boll Weevil who gets in their ears and whispers bad thoughts–things they shouldn't do, things the shouldn't think, things they shouldn't say–but are soooo tempted to do! But, they also learn that they hold the key to the remedy for this loathsome pest–a little prayer that can chase him away.

ISBN: 0-78144-063-7   ITEM #: 103315   10 x 8   HC   36P

## Humble Bee
*A Story about Pride*

Have you learned that your friends don't like your bragging? Humble Bee was a bee who bragged. He made bee-licious snacks that everyone loved–but his boasting created a big problem, and children can learn from his story that everyone should be humble.

ISBN: 0-78143-831-4   ITEM #: 101761   10 x 8   HC   32P

## The Non-Praying Mantis
*A Story about Prayer and Thankfulness*

Have you ever asked God for something but didn't get it? After a big disappointment, the Non-Praying Mantis finally discovers the secret of seeing her prayers answered. Children will learn the valuable lesson that, even when they don't get the answer they want, it's important to talk to God.

ISBN: 0-78143-830-6   ITEM #: 101762   10 x 8   HC   32P

## The GigANTic Little Hero
*A Story about Perseverance*

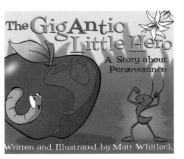

An ant who lacks confidence seeks the aid of a spider and a grasshopper to carry a heavy load. When they suddenly leave him, he's unaware that he's carrying the weight all alone! He learns he CAN do the job, which builds his confidence and courage, and through his story, children will see that they too can have the confidence to do any task!

ISBN: 0-78143-517-X   ITEM #: 99929   10 x 8   HC   32P

## Order Your Copies Today!

Order Online: www.cookministries.com, Phone: 1-800-323-7543, or Visit your local Christian bookstore

# The Word at Work Around the World

What would you do if you wanted to share God's love with children on the streets of your city? That's the dilemma David C. Cook faced in 1870's Chicago. His answer was to create literature that would capture children's hearts.

Out of those humble beginnings grew a worldwide ministry that has used literature to proclaim God's love and disciple generation after generation. Cook Communications Ministries is committed to personal discipleship—to helping people of all ages learn God's Word, embrace his salvation, walk in his ways, and minister in his name.

Faith Kidz, RiverOak, Honor, Life Journey, Victor, NextGen . . . every time you purchase a book produced by Cook Communications Ministries, you not only meet a vital personal need in your life or in the life of someone you love, but you're also a part of ministering to José in Colombia, Humberto in Chile, Gousa in India, or Lidiane in Brazil. You help make it possible for a pastor in China, a child in Peru, or a mother in West Africa to enjoy a life-changing book. And because you helped, children and adults around the world are learning God's Word and walking in his ways.

Thank you for your partnership in helping to disciple the world. May God bless you with the power of his Word in your life.

*For more information about our international ministries,*
*visit www.ccmi.org.*